Ballet

PAS DE QUATRE

Divertissement. *Choreography by Jules Perrot. Music by Cesare Pugni. First presented July 12, 1845 at Her Majesty's Theatre, London, with Marie Taglioni, Fanny Cerrito, Lucille Grahn and Carlotta Grisi.*

This short ballet displayed the exceptional talents of four of the greatest ballerinas of the period. It is probably the most famous *divertissement* (a dance for simple diversion or pleasure).

Color & Story

Written by KAY TICHENOR

Illustrated by HELEN KUNIC

 TROUBADOR PRESS
a subsidiary of
PRICE/STERN/SLOAN
Publishers, Inc., Los Angeles
1986

The Court Ballet

Primitive man danced by instinct and his movements were representative of what he saw, felt and experienced. As time passed, civilized man and his dance became more refined. Dance became part of religious and social life. Priests were chosen to dramatize through dance what were meant to be godlike gestures and movements. Folk dancing, a skill popular with the people, is a part of the heritage of every country. Dance as an art for entertainment grew out of the Greek dramas which included singing, pantomime and meaningful movement as a part of the storytelling. Pantomime, or mime, comes from the Greek word *pantomimos,* meaning all-imitating. It is a means of expression using gestures and signs with no words. It has become ballet's way of communicating complicated parts of the story.

The ancient Romans combined mime and dance with acrobatics and circus routines as a way of illustrating popular fables. Actors with masks were a popular part of dramatic presentations in civilized countries of western Europe known as mummings or masquerades.

Ballet emerged as a distinctive form in the 15th century at the Renaissance courts of Italy. The first ballet on record was in 1489, in honor of the Duke of Milan's wedding to Isabel of Aragon. In Milan as well, Leonardo da Vinci painted scenes for the great religious ballets. Ballet comes from the Italian *ballare,* which means to dance. An art without nationality, ballet has more of a family history. Dancers learn basic steps and movements from a teacher who was a student of an earlier master, often from another country.

Court dances, called *balletti* (little dance), included graceful movements of the head, arms and top of the body, with small delicate leg movements creating elaborate floor patterns and rhythms. Dancers were limited by their clothes made with heavy fabrics and ornaments weighing as much as 150 pounds. The cumbersome costumes set off the tiny feet and elegant waists of the women, and the supple legs, insteps and hands of the men, who were usually accomplished swordsmen.

Catherine de Medici married Henry of Orleans (later Henry II) in 1533 and took Italian pageantry to France. She commissioned *La Ballet Comique de la Reine* in 1581. Often called the first modern ballet, it was choreographed by Balthazar de Beaujoyeulx, lasted five to six hours, and made Catherine the envy of other European royal houses. Choreography, from the Greek words *choreos* (dance) and *grapho* (record), means to record dance patterns or to create dances.

Ballet and music were part of the great court spectacles which also included poetry, songs and even choreography on horseback! Riders guided their horses through intricate formations.

During the 17th century ballet flourished in France. Louis XIV, himself a dancer and named the Sun King for a role he played, founded the Royal Ballet Academy in 1661, the Royal Music Academy eight years later and the National Ballet School in 1672. The universally accepted language of dance is French. Early dancers were men in masks, performing dances complex in pattern and floor design with themes about everyday events.

Louis XIV's dancing master and the first ballet master of the Academy, Pierre Beauchamp, established the Five Positions of the feet that became the basis for training at the Academy and for all performance. Dance had become more than a courtly pastime. It had become a profession and had developed into a serious and responsible art expression. Ballet was distinguished from all other forms of theatrical dance by the Five Positions with emphasis on the turned-out leg. The legs are turned out from the hip at an angle of ninety degrees, a position that was not perfected until dancers removed the heels from their shoes. Although the position allows amazing dexterity and balance, students are never pushed to achieve complete turnout without thorough preparation.

Jean Baptiste Lully, who was a dancer, composer, violinist, conductor, and even stage manager, wrote the music and presented *The Triumph of Love,* the first ballet with trained women, for the court at Versailles in 1681. It featured Mademoiselle Lafontaine as the first *première danseuse* (leading female dancer). Its public performance in Paris in 1708 established ballet as a separate art, and dance continued to develop apart from court entertainment, drama and opera.

Lully was succeeded by a man who encouraged his dancers to aim at dancing off the floor. Lully had seen dancing move from the ballroom to the stage but he had only been concerned with dance that was on the same level as the spectators and imitated ballroom technique. His successor, Rameau, realized that the raised stage made a difference. The dancer's feet were now visible, which called for a difference in technique. So began disagreement between tradition and innovation that has continued through the history of ballet to the present.

ISBN: 0-8431-1718-4

La Sylphide

Ballet in two acts. Choreography by Filippo Taglioni. Music by Jean Schneitzhoeffer. Book by Adolphe Hourrit. Scenery by Pierre Ciceri. Costumes by Eugene Lami. First presented at the Théâtre de l'Académie Royale de Musique, Paris, March 12, 1832, with Marie Taglioni as La Sylphide. Presented by the Royal Danish Ballet in 1836 in a version choreographed by Auguste Bournonville with music by Herman Lovenskjold. Lucille Grahn danced the title role.

Ballet activity grew during the 18th century in London, Milan, Copenhagen, Vienna, St. Petersburg and other great cities, but the Paris Opéra remained the capital of the ballet world.

Costumes, choreography and dance technique saw changes in the developing art form. Marie Camargo, a ballerina favored by the public, introduced the *entrechat* (jumping straight up with weaving motions of the feet) for women, shortened her dancing dress to mid-calf, wore tights for reasons of modesty, and shoes without heels. Her rival Marie Sallé wore loose hair, loose, free muslin garments draped in the Grecian style, and was the first woman choreographer.

Jean Georges Noverre, a revolutionary ballet master, described his ideas in a book, *Lettres sur la danse et les ballets,* in 1760. He wanted the ballet to tell a story (*ballet d'action*), aided by the music, decor and dance. He stressed naturalism, simplifying costumes, and abolishing the mask.

In the 19th century, the classical themes of mythological heroes were replaced by tales of fantasy and romantic folk legends. The *ballet blanc* (ballets in which girls wear long white costumes) became famous with the creation of *La Sylphide* (still popular in repertories in the United States, Canada and Europe) and the dancing of the ballerina, Marie Taglioni. Her muslin costume was as light and delicate as the fairy creature she portrayed, darting through trees and casement windows. Lami's costume design became standard, no matter what color, remaining as the romantic tutu to this day. A new technique was created when Taglioni danced on her *pointes,* or the tips of her toes for the first time.

The Romantic Age had begun and choreographers were inspired to create ballets for the famous dancers of the period. In the past, original choreography, which had been created for a special function, a court ballet or a public entertainment, was forgotten as soon as it was performed. Dancers such as Taglioni would perform a role many times, traveling throughout Europe. In this way a ballet became popular and was preserved. The dancers taught their roles to favorite pupils so that when they retired, ballets like *La Sylphide* lived on.

The story of *La Sylphide,* subtitled the *Sylph of the Highlands,* concerns a young Scotsman, James, who is about to be married to Effie. As he dozes before the fireplace, he dreams of a lovely, young creature. He awakens to find a winged sylphide on the floor at his feet, her long white dress against the bridegroom's bright tartan. She dances for James but is frightened when he reaches for her, and rushes up the chimney.

Meanwhile, his friend Gurn is disconsolate because he too loves Effie and will soon lose her to James.

James is enchanted with the vision of the wistful sylphide who returns many times during the wedding preparations and once appears in the window frame. Effie is concerned about James' behavior but does not believe Gurn's story of James' interest in another woman. The sylphide returns during the wedding ceremony and snatches the ring just as James is about to put it on Effie's finger. The guests gasp and James turns away from his bride to follow the sylphide who has said she will die if he marries someone else.

James enters the forest and is confronted by Old Madge, the village sorceress, who gives him a magic scarf, promising it will remove the sylphide's wings, so that she will belong to James forever. The sylphide approaches and he drapes the scarf about her shoulders. She clutches at her heart in mortal agony and her wings fall to the ground. She dies slowly and is carried away by her winged sisters. James falls to the ground, weeping, and the old witch exults in triumph. Gurn's and Effie's wedding procession passes in the distance to the sound of faraway church bells.

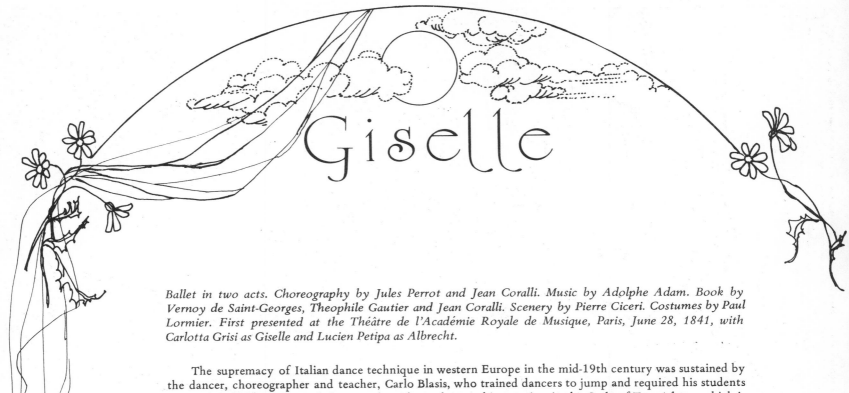

Giselle

Ballet in two acts. Choreography by Jules Perrot and Jean Coralli. Music by Adolphe Adam. Book by Vernoy de Saint-Georges, Theophile Gautier and Jean Coralli. Scenery by Pierre Ciceri. Costumes by Paul Lormier. First presented at the Théâtre de l'Académie Royale de Musique, Paris, June 28, 1841, with Carlotta Grisi as Giselle and Lucien Petipa as Albrecht.

The supremacy of Italian dance technique in western Europe in the mid-19th century was sustained by the dancer, choreographer and teacher, Carlo Blasis, who trained dancers to jump and required his students to practice daily. He stressed the turned-out leg and wrote his exercises in the *Code of Terpsichore*, which is still the basis of classical training. He developed the *attitude*, a position copied from a statue of Mercury.

The ballerina was idolized during the Romantic period and the romantic ballet was responsible for daring innovations in dance technique and subject; girls danced on their toes by strengthening the tips of the toe shoes with darning, and new steps of elevation were devised to transform real-life heroines into lighter-than-air spirit-maidens.

Salvatore Vigano produced spectacular ballets that unified music, dancing and mime, and under his direction, La Scala in Milan, Italy, became the greatest ballet theatre in all of Europe.

Giselle was created for an Italian ballerina, Carlotta Grisi, and it is just as popular today as when it was first performed. Every ballerina wants to dance the role of *Giselle*, for it is a test of her dramatic talent as well as technical ability. It is a ballet to be seen for the performance of its ballerina alone.

The role of the male dancer in the romantic ballets became merely one of supporting the ballerina; Jules Perrot was perhaps the most famous of the period.

The story of the Wilis, a German legend, seemed to be ideal for ballet. The Wilis were young girls who were engaged to be married but died before their wedding days. They rose from their graves in the evenings and danced in the moonlight, attracting their suitors to dance with them, compelling them to dance until they died.

The poets and novelists were all interested in stories of the romantically supernatural — the beautiful, unattainable sylphide who vanished when she was touched, and the mortal heroine who could be real and unreal at the same time.

Gautier read the story of the Wilis and thought it would make a good ballet for Carlotta Grisi with whom he was in love. Trained by her husband, Jules Perrot, she had become a ballerina to rival Marie Taglioni and Fanny Elssler.

The libretto, or story of the ballet, was written in three days. The lovely musical score was written within a week. At its performance *Giselle* was proclaimed the greatest ballet of its time and a triumphant successor to *La Sylphide*.

Act One takes place in a village on the Rhine. Giselle is a pretty peasant girl who is in love with Albrecht, a handsome young duke disguised as Loys, a peasant. Giselle loves to dance and is warned by her mother that her heart will fail from so much dancing and she will become one of the Wilis, doomed to dance forever, even in death. When Giselle discovers that Albrecht is not a peasant and is engaged to a Princess, her heart is broken. She is so defenseless that she loses her reason and stabs herself with Albrecht's sword.

Act Two takes place within a forest glade at midnight. The scene is misty with the dewy night. The moon penetrates the thick trees; its light is reflected in a nearby lake and in the dimness we can see Giselle's grave with her name etched on a large cross. Giselle is called forth from her grave and initiated into the Wilis. Albrecht comes to visit the grave of his beloved and Giselle is ordered by Myrtha, the Queen of the Wilis, to engage him in a dance to his death. Giselle begs that he be spared, but Myrtha refuses. Albrecht tries to seek protection from the cross on her grave but is powerless to resist Giselle, who must obey her queen. Soon they are engaged in a mad whirl and the young duke would have died from exhaustion if the church clock had not sounded the hour of four. With the approach of dawn, the Wilis slowly return to their graves. As Albrecht watches, Giselle vanishes, dancing away with his heart forever.

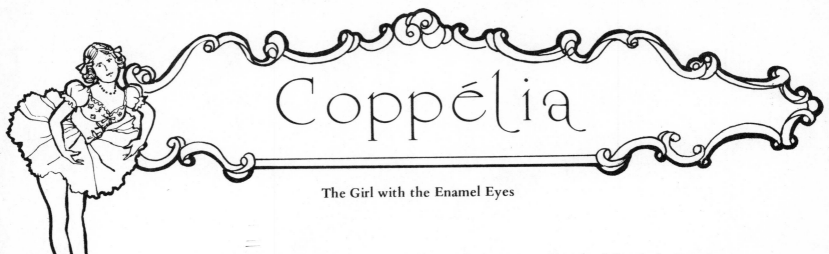

Coppélia

The Girl with the Enamel Eyes

Ballet in three acts. Choreography by Arthur Saint-Léon. Music by Léo Delibes. Book by Charles Nuitter and Arthur Saint-Léon, after a story by E. T. A. Hoffman. First presented at the Théâtre Imperiale de l'Opéra, Paris, May 25, 1870, with Guiseppina Bozacchi as Swanilda and Eugenie Fiocre as Franz.

France and Italy were the centers of ballet until the beginning of the 20th century although other European countries also enjoyed watching ballet. Auguste Bournonville in Denmark had established the Danish style of dancing which was characterized by quick, brilliant footwork. Dancers visited London to great acclaim. America had been enjoying ballet, both native and imported, for almost 100 years. Augusta Maywood danced with the Paris Opera and became the first American ballerina to be placed on a par with other European dancers by the European public.

Coppélia is one of the earliest ballets to be based on the story of a doll coming to life. It is considered to be ballet's great comedy, just as *Giselle* is the great tragedy.

The young dancer in the Paris Opera chosen to dance the role of Swanilda was just 15 years old. Reviewers praised her for her skillful dancing, her acting ability and her pretty features. Regrettably, her future as a dancer was cut short by her death from a fever during the siege of Paris at the outbreak of the Franco-Prussian War, just two months after the ballet's premiere. The role of Franz was originally danced by a ballerina and the role has been played by a woman in subsequent French revivals.

The musical score for *Coppélia* has infectious charm and gaiety and includes many attractive melodies, well suited to the dance. It was Léo Delibes' first full-length ballet. He composed *Sylvia* six years later and was soon established as one of the greatest composers in this art form. Along with Delibes' scores, Adolphe Adam's music for *Giselle* and Tchaikovsky's music for *Swan Lake, The Sleeping Beauty,* and *The Nutcracker* are enjoyed alone as well as in combination with the ballets.

This ballet tells the story of a quaint old gentleman named Dr. Coppélius, his doll Coppélia, and the sweethearts Swanilda and Franz. Coppélius is a toymaker, also said to dabble in magic, who has made a doll so life-like that he enjoys pretending she is human. He puts Coppélia in the window of his house, her glazed enamel-blue eyes staring at the reactions of passing folk. Franz is a young villager taken in by her natural appearance, much to the annoyance of his true love, Swanilda. She has observed Franz blowing kisses to the doll. Coppélia appears to wave encouragement to him, but the mischievous Dr. Coppélius, hiding behind her, is moving her arm.

Although infatuated with the mysterious lady in the window, Franz loves Swanilda, and is very disappointed when she refuses his proposal of marriage. He determines to ask Coppélia that night to marry him.

That evening old Dr. Coppélius decides to stretch his spindly legs in a walk around the village square. He locks his door with a large key and totters off, straight into a mob of pranksters. In the encounter he doesn't notice that he has dropped his key.

Swanilda and her friends find the key to the toymaker's door. She realizes this is a chance to discover the secrets of her rival's charm. They all troop into the toymaker's workshop.

In the dim light the girls are startled at first and then delighted to find a marvelous collection of mechanical figures. They wind the keys to set the figures in motion, while Swanilda searches for Coppélia. When the doll does not return her polite greeting, Swanilda sees that she is no more real than any of the other toys in the workshop.

A furious Dr. Coppélius returns and chases the girls away, all but the hidden Swanilda. At this moment Franz, who has climbed up a ladder, enters the room. Upon hearing his confession of love, Dr. Coppélius offers him a glass of wine. Franz soon falls asleep, and the old toymaker decides to search his magic books for a way to give Franz's life to Coppélia.

Swanilda has put on Coppélia's clothes and the old man, with his failing eyesight, is deceived. He believes his enchantment has worked when the doll begins to move, walk and dance. Swanilda cooperates with his direction, executing a Spanish bolero and a Scottish reel. She soon tires of the game, begins to destroy his workshop, and finally drags Franz home.

Franz is ashamed that he has been fooled by a sawdust doll and again asks Swanilda to be his wife. Now she agrees, knowing that she will never again have a rival.

The Sleeping Beauty

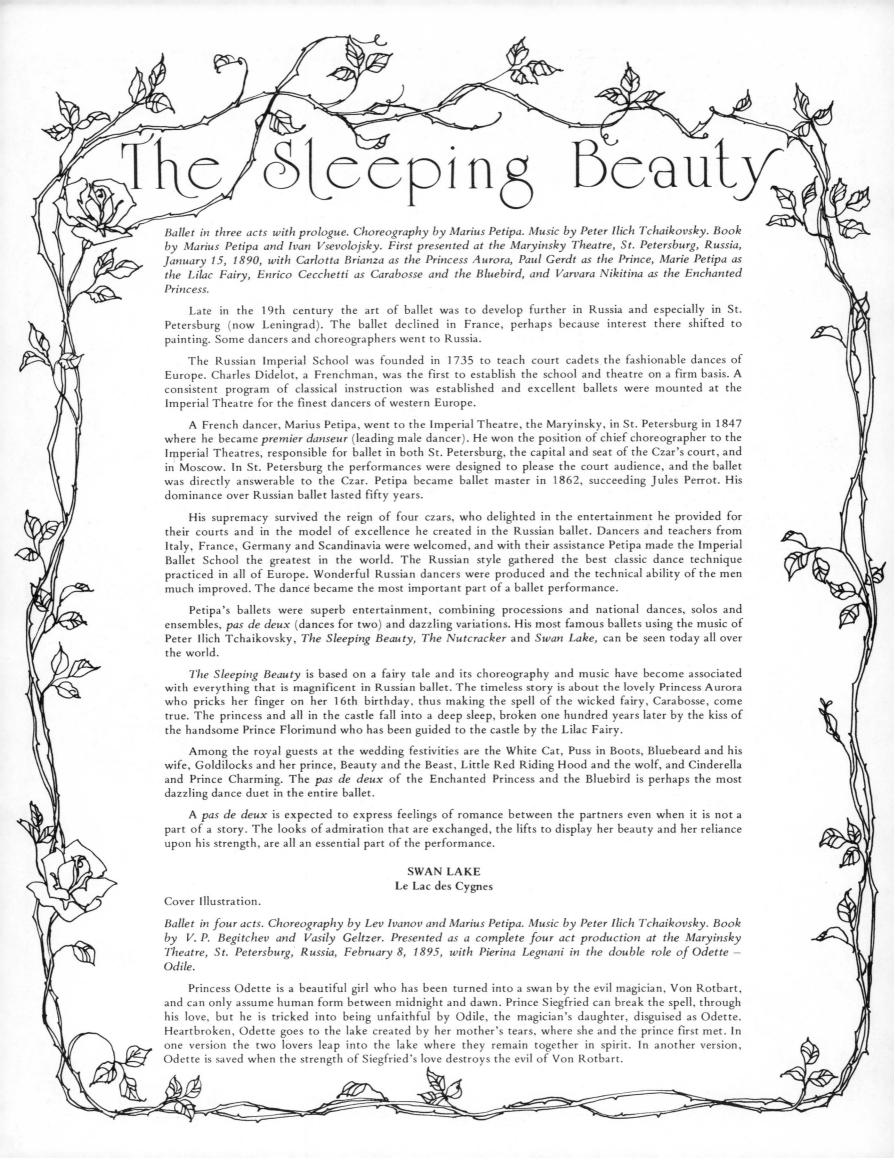

Ballet in three acts with prologue. Choreography by Marius Petipa. Music by Peter Ilich Tchaikovsky. Book by Marius Petipa and Ivan Vsevolojsky. First presented at the Maryinsky Theatre, St. Petersburg, Russia, January 15, 1890, with Carlotta Brianza as the Princess Aurora, Paul Gerdt as the Prince, Marie Petipa as the Lilac Fairy, Enrico Cecchetti as Carabosse and the Bluebird, and Varvara Nikitina as the Enchanted Princess.

Late in the 19th century the art of ballet was to develop further in Russia and especially in St. Petersburg (now Leningrad). The ballet declined in France, perhaps because interest there shifted to painting. Some dancers and choreographers went to Russia.

The Russian Imperial School was founded in 1735 to teach court cadets the fashionable dances of Europe. Charles Didelot, a Frenchman, was the first to establish the school and theatre on a firm basis. A consistent program of classical instruction was established and excellent ballets were mounted at the Imperial Theatre for the finest dancers of western Europe.

A French dancer, Marius Petipa, went to the Imperial Theatre, the Maryinsky, in St. Petersburg in 1847 where he became *premier danseur* (leading male dancer). He won the position of chief choreographer to the Imperial Theatres, responsible for ballet in both St. Petersburg, the capital and seat of the Czar's court, and in Moscow. In St. Petersburg the performances were designed to please the court audience, and the ballet was directly answerable to the Czar. Petipa became ballet master in 1862, succeeding Jules Perrot. His dominance over Russian ballet lasted fifty years.

His supremacy survived the reign of four czars, who delighted in the entertainment he provided for their courts and in the model of excellence he created in the Russian ballet. Dancers and teachers from Italy, France, Germany and Scandinavia were welcomed, and with their assistance Petipa made the Imperial Ballet School the greatest in the world. The Russian style gathered the best classic dance technique practiced in all of Europe. Wonderful Russian dancers were produced and the technical ability of the men much improved. The dance became the most important part of a ballet performance.

Petipa's ballets were superb entertainment, combining processions and national dances, solos and ensembles, *pas de deux* (dances for two) and dazzling variations. His most famous ballets using the music of Peter Ilich Tchaikovsky, *The Sleeping Beauty, The Nutcracker* and *Swan Lake,* can be seen today all over the world.

The Sleeping Beauty is based on a fairy tale and its choreography and music have become associated with everything that is magnificent in Russian ballet. The timeless story is about the lovely Princess Aurora who pricks her finger on her 16th birthday, thus making the spell of the wicked fairy, Carabosse, come true. The princess and all in the castle fall into a deep sleep, broken one hundred years later by the kiss of the handsome Prince Florimund who has been guided to the castle by the Lilac Fairy.

Among the royal guests at the wedding festivities are the White Cat, Puss in Boots, Bluebeard and his wife, Goldilocks and her prince, Beauty and the Beast, Little Red Riding Hood and the wolf, and Cinderella and Prince Charming. The *pas de deux* of the Enchanted Princess and the Bluebird is perhaps the most dazzling dance duet in the entire ballet.

A *pas de deux* is expected to express feelings of romance between the partners even when it is not a part of a story. The looks of admiration that are exchanged, the lifts to display her beauty and her reliance upon his strength, are all an essential part of the performance.

SWAN LAKE
Le Lac des Cygnes

Cover Illustration.

Ballet in four acts. Choreography by Lev Ivanov and Marius Petipa. Music by Peter Ilich Tchaikovsky. Book by V. P. Begitchev and Vasily Geltzer. Presented as a complete four act production at the Maryinsky Theatre, St. Petersburg, Russia, February 8, 1895, with Pierina Legnani in the double role of Odette — Odile.

Princess Odette is a beautiful girl who has been turned into a swan by the evil magician, Von Rotbart, and can only assume human form between midnight and dawn. Prince Siegfried can break the spell, through his love, but he is tricked into being unfaithful by Odile, the magician's daughter, disguised as Odette. Heartbroken, Odette goes to the lake created by her mother's tears, where she and the prince first met. In one version the two lovers leap into the lake where they remain together in spirit. In another version, Odette is saved when the strength of Siegfried's love destroys the evil of Von Rotbart.

Cinderella

Ballet in three acts. Choreography by Frederick Ashton. Music by Sergei Prokofiev. Scenery and costumes by Jean-Denis Malches. First presented by the Sadler's Wells Ballet at the Royal Opera House, Covent Garden, London, December 23, 1948, with Moira Shearer as Cinderella, Michael Somes as the Prince, Robert Helpmann and Frederick Ashton as the Stepsisters. There was an earlier version in 1893, choreographed by Marius Petipa, Lev Ivanov and Enrico Cecchetti. The Bolshoi Ballet presented a version in Moscow in 1945, with Prokofiev's music.

By the end of the 19th century the blocked toe shoe had appeared. The end of this shoe is stiffened with glue and canvas, makes a knocking sound and weighs several ounces more than a soft ballet shoe. Marie Taglioni's shoes were nearly weightless and soundless. Only circus riders and music hall performers stiffened their shoes artificially prior to the 20th century, a practice that was considered a vulgar display.

Ballet dresses had come to reflect the nature of the roles for which they are still used today. The bell-shaped romantic tutu, popularized by Marie Taglioni, is considered suitable for lyrical, romantic dancing. The classical tutu, an extremely short and stiff skirt with a layer of frills, was also in use by the end of the 19th century, providing freedom of movement for more virtuoso dancing, which can be a more vigorous display of technique.

The code of ballet as a dance form — which today is identical all over the world — was formulated by 1820, and has remained essentially the same ever since. The instructions for this code were written by Carlo Blasis, who assembled the basic theories of great dancers preceding him. His work is still the foundation of all instruction in classic dance, although certain national characteristics had begun to develop during the 19th century. The Italians stressed accomplished footwork and *pirouettes* (complete turns of the body on one foot), but neglected jumps. Both French and Italians were particular about arm movements (*port de bras*), allowing little freedom from tradition. The Danes were more romantic and free, and developed acting techniques. The Russians were more vigorous, adding higher kicks. The 19th century styles, however, were basically mild, with the accent on lightness and nimble footwork. Characteristics that have been added in the 20th century include showy pointwork made possible by the stiffened shoe, acrobatic lifts and more realistic acting. In a continuous link with history, the graceful dancer of today correctly places her head, arms and hands in the style of the 17th century court dancer, whose arms and hands were forced into the curved position by the continual lifting of heavy costumes.

Cinderella has appeared in a variety of styles, since the ballet has attracted many choreographers — French, Russian, English and American. The best known early ballet version was that of Marius Petipa in Russia in 1893. The best known productions today are those with music by the Russian composer, Sergei Prokofiev. He conceived *Cinderella* "as a classical ballet with variations [dances for one person], *adagios* [dances in a slow tempo by a ballerina and her partner], *pas de deux* [dance for two people], etc. I see Cinderella not only as a fairytale character but also as a real person, feeling, experiencing, and moving among us." He began work on the score in 1940 and completed the orchestration in 1944.

The folk tale dates back to 9th century China and was included in the collections of both Charles Perrault and the Grimm brothers. According to the tale, a young girl is destined for a life of drudgery by a heartless stepmother and two vain, haughty stepsisters. Cinderella is expected to live and work with the servants in the household. She has been given her name because her clothes are stained by the cinders and soot from the hearth of the fireplace. When she is disappointed that she is unable to attend the Prince's ball with her stepsisters, a fairy godmother appears and with her magic wand transforms Cinderella into a beautiful Princess with a lovely gown and glass slippers. Cinderella goes to the ball and delights the Prince while others wonder who she is. She has been warned by her fairy godmother to leave before twelve o'clock or her coach would change back to a pumpkin, each horse would change back to a mouse, the young men at the back of the coach would become lizards, and her fine clothes would again be rags. Cinderella is so happy dancing with the Prince that she forgets about time. When she hears the clock striking twelve, she hastily leaves the palace, losing one of her glass slippers on the staircase. The Prince finds it and vows to find the girl whom it fits and make her his bride. All the young girls in the land try on the slipper but it fits only Cinderella. She and the Prince are wed and live happily ever after.

Les Sylphides

Classic ballet in one act. Choreography by Michel Fokine. Music by Frédéric Chopin. First presented by Serge Diaghilev's Ballets Russes at the Théâtre de Châtelet, Paris, June 2, 1909, with Anna Pavlova, Tamara Karsavina, Alexandra Baldina, and Vaslav Nijinsky as the principal dancers.

At the turn of the century, a girl from Oakland, California, Isadora Duncan, threw off the restrictions of corset and shoes, and danced barefoot. At this same time, companies in Europe were becoming dissatisfied with classical ballet and were attempting new styles of choreography. American dancers complained that ballet rules were stiff and unnatural and that it was impossible to express inspiration because of concern over accuracy of technique.

Isadora Duncan placed dancing on a par with religion, stressing dance as a form of worship and as the mother of the arts. She performed without scenery, using only curtains and lights. She wore simple tunics and scarves and danced only to the best music. She felt that dancing was proper for everyone, regardless of class or social standing.

Isadora Duncan had her strongest professional influence in Europe, where a 25 year-old Russian dancer and choreographer, Michel Fokine, was greatly impressed. Although he was a product of the Imperial Ballet School in St. Petersburg and a pupil of Marius Petipa's, he rebelled against the power of tradition and aimed for the unification of dancing, music and design. Like Noverre 160 years earlier, and Jules Perrot, Fokine wanted many reforms including a unity of emotional expression throughout a ballet. One of Fokine's innovations was to enhance the role of the *Corps De Ballet,* the "chorus" of the ballet company. Before the 20th century its function was merely decorative. He insisted that no dance number be used unless it served the overall dramatic purpose of the choreography. He discarded rigid patterns, worked without formulas and used any order or sequence that told the story best. Isadora Duncan's influence on Fokine was evident in his efforts to use simple means to depict feelings and sentiments.

Les Sylphides is generally regarded as a typically romantic ballet and as Fokine's masterpiece. It has a dream-like atmosphere: the ballerinas are in long white dresses, and the danseur (male soloist) is in black and white velvet. The music of Chopin is played and the settings are purely romantic.

Les Sylphides (spirits of the air) is the 20th century namesake of *La Sylphide* and restored the idea of the *ballet blanc* which had passed out of fashion. For more than half a century, ballets had been more concerned with dancing than with mood, and with elaborate stage spectacles, instead of with simple stories of fantasy and ethereal romance. The term *ballet blanc* describes a ballet containing more dance than pantomime and in which the women wear white tutus. The second act of *Swan Lake,* for example, frequently appears in repertories independently of the complete ballet and is known as a *ballet blanc.*

An earlier version of *Les Sylphides* appeared in 1907 as *Chopiniana,* and was based on a legendary incident in the life of Chopin. Three choreographic versions later, *Les Sylphides* was presented in Paris, in 1909, with the name changed on advice of the painter, Alexander Benois, who thought it would cause people to associate the ballet with the romantic story of *La Sylphide.* The ballet has been staged in many versions and, since its first performance in Paris, has become a part of the repertory of most large companies. The first performance in the United States was presented at the Winter Garden, New York, June 14, 1911, with Alexandra Baldina as one of the principal dancers. Baldina, who also performed in the premier performance in Paris, 1909, was trained at the Imperial Ballet School in St. Petersburg and danced at the Maryinsky Theatre.

When the curtain rises for this ballet, the dancers are seen against the backdrop of a moonlit forest and a castle in ruins. The ensemble dances a nocturne (a composition of dreamy, night-like mood), followed by one soloist dancing a waltz (a popular dance in three-quarter time), another dancing a mazurka (a stately Polish national dance), and then comes a second mazurka solo by the *danseur.* The prelude (an introductory section) is danced by a third female soloist followed by her *pas de deux* with the male soloist. The *corps de ballet* stands in groups on the stage, changing its position from time to time. The *corps de ballet* presents a waltz and at its climax the soloists appear on the stage. Finally there is a return to the original grouping, and as the curtain falls, the entire ensemble is in the same position as at the beginning. It is as if a dream had briefly come to life.

The Nutcracker Ballet

Ballet in two acts. Choreography begun by Marius Petipa, completed by Lev Ivanov. Music by Peter Ilich Tchaikovsky. Book by Marius Petipa. Scenery by M. I. Botcharov. First presented at the Maryinsky Theatre, St. Petersburg, December 17, 1892, with Antoinetta Dell-Era and Paul Gerdt as the Sugarplum Fairy and the Prince.

The Story of *The Nutcracker* begins at the home of the Burgomaster, an important man, who always entertains his family and close friends with a grand party on Christmas Eve. The Burgomaster has two children, Clara and Fritz. The party is mostly for them and their friends. The guests arrive, marveling at the large lighted tree. The children speculate about the presents and the governess arranges games and dances.

The children's godfather, Herr Drosselmeyer, arrives late to the party. He has brought mechanical dolls to dance for the children. Herr Drosselmeyer has a special gift for Clara, a toy nutcracker. Teasing brother Fritz causes a squabble, breaks the nutcracker, and Clara bursts into tears.

After everyone has gone to bed, Clara tiptoes into the living room, finds her beloved toy and cradles it in her arms. She is startled to be confronted by a live nutcracker doll, who then must lead the toy soldiers in a losing battle against a horde of invading mice. Clara throws her slipper at the Mouse King and the battle is won.

The nutcracker is transformed into a handsome young prince who invites Clara to come with him to the Land of Sweets. They travel through the Kingdom of Snow where the Snow King and Queen and the Snowflakes dance for them.

They arrive at the palace of the Sugarplum Fairy who organizes a festival in their honor. The drinks and candies that children love come to life and dance: Spanish chocolate, Arabian coffee, Chinese tea, candy canes, candy bonbons in lovely pastel colors, Mother Ginger and her children, candy flowers and finally the most beautiful dance of all by the Sugarplum Fairy and her cavalier. Sadly, Clara bids them a reluctant farewell and leaves with the Nutcracker Prince.

Petrouchka

Ballet in one act, four scenes. Choreography by Michel Fokine. Music by Igor Stravinsky. Book by Stravinsky and Alexander Benois. First presented by Diaghilev's Ballets Russes at the Théâtre du Châtelet, Paris, June 13, 1911, with Vaslav Nijinsky as Petrouchka, Tamara Karsavina as the Ballerina, Alexandre Orlov as the Moor and Enrico Cecchetti as the Charlatan.

The choreographic reforms suggested by Michel Fokine were not accepted by his superiors at the Imperial Theatre in St. Petersburg. These reforms, however, were appreciated by others like Serge Diaghilev, an art critic, and graduate of St. Petersburg Conservatory of Music, who had a fine understanding of music, painting and dancing. He had presented Russian music to western Europe for the first time in 1907, and he wanted the Europeans to enjoy what he knew to be the finest dancers in the world. He formed a company in Paris known as Diaghilev's Ballets Russes and chose Fokine as the choreographer. His principal dancers secured leave from the Imperial Theatre. The first season opened in 1909, and for the next 20 years the Ballets Russes presented dance entertainment with unexcelled choreography, music, decor and performance.

Petrouchka is one of the greatest repertory dance-dramas in the world, and is a good example of the unity which can result when all members of the creative team work together on equal terms. It began as a musical idea. The composer, Stravinsky, wanted to write a piece for piano and orchestra in which the piano would be attacked by the mass of instruments. In his mind he had an image of the piano as being represented by a puppet. The word to express his image was "Petrouchka, the immortal and unhappy hero of every fair." Diaghilev liked Stravinsky's idea and the ballet went into production.

Petrouchka is ballet's representation of a universal character in the popular theatrical tradition of Europe for hundreds of years — the half comic, half tragic clown who is never taken seriously, the unlucky funny man who is usually wiser than anyone else.

This character was an outgrowth of the comic art of the ancient Roman tumblers, jesters and buffoons. This art form was reborn in 16th century Italy in troupes of traveling entertainers. Known as *commedia dell'arte,* the skilled comedians improvised favorite characters in familiar plots. Their gestures, costumes and characterizations influenced dancers, playwrights and carnival puppet shows. The creators of *Petrouchka* had enjoyed in their youth the "Russian Punch and Judy Show."

In ballet prior to Fokine the stage was divided into separate dancing areas for the *corps de ballet,* the soloists and the ballerinas. The patterns were seldom changed. With Fokine, in developing the principle of expressiveness, each dancer contributed vitally to the general impression. In the original production of *Petrouchka,* every dancer in the crowd scene had something to do at every moment in many areas of the stage, and each dancer was related in both action and reaction to the principal dancers.

Petrouchka has been described as a choreographic masterpiece for which it is impossible to relate the vivid sense of life animating the whole ballet. Nijinsky's performance as Petrouchka was described as perhaps his most wonderful achievement. His facial expression, as a puppet, never changed — the character was portrayed only in the action of movement. Yet the expression of grief was vividly communicated to the audience.

The ballet is set in the middle of a noisy Russian fair on a winter day around 1830 just before Lent. The principal characters are three puppets — Petrouchka and the Moor, who are both in love with the Ballerina.

Merry-makers mingle in the snow-covered square — peasants, gypsies, soldiers and well-dressed folk all in holiday attire. A variety of festive activities are taking place and are accentuated by the merriment of the music with its quick changing rhythms. The crowd is attracted to one booth where three puppets perform on command of a showman, the Charlatan. The puppets dance mechanically to an energetic, demanding tempo and act out a drama of flirtation, jealousy and rage, until they are commanded to stop.

After the show, behind the scenes, the drama is reenacted, although they are only puppets imitating human expression. Petrouchka is unable to compete with the Moor for the affection of the Ballerina and in private, as on stage, always loses. In truth the Ballerina cares little for either of them. But Petrouchka imagines that she is suffering at the hands of the powerful Moor, and gamely attempts a gallant rescue. The Moor is enraged, draws his scimitar (curved sword), and chases the defenseless Petrouchka out into the square. Petrouchka is overtaken by the Moor and struck down with one blow. His wooden body is reduced to splinters. The confused crowd thinks a crime has been committed. The policeman is persuaded by the Charlatan that Petrouchka was never more than a lifeless doll. But the ghost of Petrouchka appears on the roof of the theatre to haunt the Charlatan and anyone else who will not believe that he is real.

La Boutique Fantasque

The Fantastic Toyshop

Ballet in one act. Choreography by Leonide Massine. Music by Gioacchino Rossini, arranged and orchestrated by Ottorina Respighi. Scenery and costumes by Andre Derain. First presented by Diaghilev's Ballets Russes at the Alhambra Theatre, London, June 5, 1919, with Enrico Cecchetti as the Shopkeeper, Lydia Lopokova and Leonide Massine as the Cancan Dancers.

With the success of Diaghilev's Ballets Russes, Paris was again the world capital of dance. The company provided a center of artistic endeavor not known to Europe since the courts of the Renaissance. Diaghilev—like the Renaissance princes —discovered, encouraged, developed and perpetuated talent among dancers, composers, artists and choreographers.

Leonide Massine succeeded Fokine and Nijinsky as master choreographer. He joined the Ballets Russes in 1913, having been discovered by Diaghilev at the Moscow Imperial School for the Theatre, where he was a student of drama and ballet. A young and promising dancer, he continued to study dance under Enrico Cecchetti, while Diaghilev encouraged his attempts at dance composition.

La Boutique Fantasque was one of the first of Massine's many productions. His early works were examples of *ballet d'action* (ballets with a story), full of unique characters with individual attitudes, movements and facial make-up. Probably he was influenced by his studies of commedia dell'arte. Most of Massine's early ballets were characterized by angular lines and a jerky, distorted style of movement as opposed to the curved lines and flowing movement associated with Fokine's choreography.

Like *Coppélia, La Boutique Fantasque* is also based on the charm of the mechanical doll. The subject was borrowed from an old German ballet. The choreography was based on the period of 1865, but the setting was inspired by the drawings and lithographs of Toulouse-Lautrec. A French painter and graphic artist of the late 1800's, Henri de Toulouse-Lautrec frequently used the cancan dancers of the Parisian dance halls as subjects. The dance involved continuous high-kicking with the raising of skirts, and was considered most daring.

The Fantastic Toyshop has been a favorite with audiences all over the world. It is filled with good humor, joy and happiness, pleasing those seriously devoted to dancing and those just seeking an evening of fun.

The Cancan Dancer doll is totally different from the stiffly-jointed puppet Ballerina in *Petrouchka*. The beloved china dolls of Victorian era children were suggested by her pouting curved lips, innocent expression, full cheeks, pale face and rounded limbs.

The ballet takes place in a great toyshop in southern France, where dolls from all over the world entertain customers from all over the world. Two English ladies and an American family with two children are entertained by peasant dolls dancing a lively tarantella, followed by dolls representing the Queen of Clubs, the Queen of Hearts, the King of Diamonds and the King of Spades, dancing a mazurka. The next dolls to perform portray a snob and a melon peddler. Their routine is a mechanical miracle and everyone in the shop enthusiastically greets the arrival of new customers, a Russian couple with four children. Five Cossack dolls perform a rapid dance and then two dancing poodles prance on their hind legs.

The prospective customers are treated to a performance by the most ingenious dolls in the shop — the cancan dancers. The girl doll abandons herself in the dance and her partner performs marvelous gravity-defying tricks. The American family decides to buy the male doll while the Russian children prefer the girl doll. They pay for their purchases and arrange to call for them the following day.

That night in the toyshop, all the dolls begin to dance again and delight in their freedom, but then feel sad that the cancan dancers are to be separated. In the morning the shop is opened and all is in order. But when the families call for the dolls, the carefully wrapped boxes are opened and are found to be empty. The children and their furious parents spring upon the poor old shopkeeper and then proceed to attack the dolls. But to their surprise the dolls come to the shopkeeper's rescue and the irate customers are finally driven from the shop by a bayonet charge of the Cossacks.

The unbelieving families peer in the windows to witness a happy dance of the triumphant dolls and the shopkeeper.

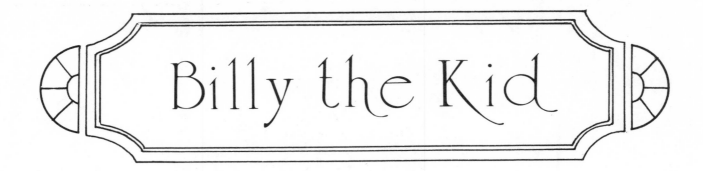

Billy the Kid

Ballet in one act. Choreography by Eugene Loring. Music by Aaron Copland. Book by Lincoln Kirstein. Scenery and costumes by Jared Franch. First presented by Ballet Caravan at the Chicago Opera House, Chicago, October 16, 1938 with Eugene Loring as Billy, Marie-Jeanne as the Mother, Lew Christensen as Pat Garrett, and Todd Bolender as Alias.

With Diaghilev's death in 1929, the Ballets Russes disbanded and his dancers and choreographers scattered, influencing ballet all over the world.

Anna Pavlova, whose name is the most famous in the ballet of the 20th century, took part in the sensational first Paris season of the Ballets Russes. In 1913, she resigned from the Maryinsky Theatre in St. Petersburg and from then until her death in 1931, she toured the world with her own company. She danced wherever there was a stage and was seen by millions. For many she was the first contact with an art that had been reserved for great cities and theatres. She first appeared in *Coppélia* in New York, and was at once a star. Following a second trip to New York, she toured the country extensively. Through her performances, Anna Pavlova taught Americans to love and respect dance.

Diaghilev and Nijinsky also opened up new ballet territory in America. A succession of dancers and companies began to tour the country. One of these was George Balanchine, a Russian choreographer from the Imperial Ballet School and the Maryinsky Theatre, who joined Diaghilev's Ballets Russes in 1925. In 1929 he became ballet master with the Royal Danish Ballet, Copenhagen, which with the Paris Opera, has the oldest continuous tradition of instruction and performance in the world. He was invited to the United States by Lincoln Kirstein to found a ballet school and in 1934, the School of American Ballet was opened in New York City.

A group briefly known as Ballet Caravan produced *Billy the Kid,* the first authentic American masterpiece. Several companies, founded and directed by Lincoln Kirstein and George Balanchine evolved into the New York City Ballet in 1948.

The story of Billy the Kid is a legend in America. His real name was William H. Bonney. He was born in New York in 1859 and was taken to Kansas when he was three. He had killed his first man when he was twelve and by the time he was fatally shot at the age of twenty-one, he had supposedly killed a man for each year of his life. An unlucky bullet that killed his mother was one of the reasons he became a desperado. He was loved and admired by some as much as he was feared by others. The ballet is not a simple biography of a Wild West killer. This heroic myth is part of the life of his time.

Ballets which incorporate American characteristics and folk dance styles with accepted classical ballet technique are a 20th century development. In *Billy the Kid, pirouettes* and double air turns are excitingly adapted to the needs of a lawless braggart of the Old West. Cowboys don't do air turns. But the movement strongly and clearly represents the attitude of bravado characteristic of Billy. The gunmen of the Old West drew fast and would sometimes spin the gun before firing in a display of arrogant fearlessness. In the ballet, Billy doesn't spin the gun, he spins himself.

The ballet begins with men and women passing slowly from left to right across a bare landscape dotted with cactus in the background — American pioneers going West.

The next scene takes place on a hot main street of an early Western town, just north of the Mexican border. There are Mexicans, pioneer women, cowboys and dancing girls. An attractive woman dressed in city clothes enters with a big, gangling boy in overalls and a straw hat who is Billy. A brawl breaks out and Billy's mother is accidentally shot by one of the Mexicans. Billy grabs a knife and without hesitation kills the Mexican and then, ignoring help, runs away. The Mexican becomes Alias and will reappear in many disguises throughout the ballet to haunt Billy.

When Billy appears again he has grown up. He dances alone, practicing preparations for the next time he will have to kill. His dance gesture for shooting is a quick aim at the target, a spin in the air that represents the speed of a bullet and finally a vicious kick.

A posse captures Billy and he is taken to jail. During a card game with the jailer, Billy grabs the gun and escapes. He returns to his hideout. Billy is tired and dances with his sweetheart as if in a dream.

Pat Garrett, led by a guide known as Alias, watches Billy sleep. Billy wakes, reaches for his gun, but sees nothing in the darkness. He lights a cigarette, illuminating his face for a moment. Garrett fires. Billy falls dead. Mourning women pass by.

The ballet ends as it began with American pioneers moving westward.

Fancy Free

Ballet in one act. Choreography by Jerome Robbins. Music by Leonard Bernstein. Scenery by Oliver Smith. Costumes by Kermit Love. First presented by Ballet Theatre at the Metropolitan Opera House, New York, April 18, 1944, with John Kriza, Harold Lang and Jerome Robbins as the three Sailors, Muriel Bentley, Janet Reed and Shirley Eckl as three Passers-by.

The early companies in the United States were formed by outstanding Russians. Most of the performers were also from Russia, although they were soon supplemented by dancers trained in America. During the thirties and the forties, most of the companies presented the romantic repertory and the Diaghilev ballets. Finally two groups emerged which developed their own tendencies — American Ballet Theatre and New York City Ballet.

Over the years American Ballet Theatre has built a repertory to include dramatic ballets on American subjects, danced to music by American composers. The works of Agnes de Mille and Jerome Robbins have had a special significance in the development of an American national ballet depicting American life in this art form.

The ballets of George Balanchine, who directs New York City Ballet, are devoted to the importance of the classic dance with no theme or dramatic incident to detract from the beauty of the dance itself. His dances are also called music ballets because the music provides the theme to which the dancers move.

Fancy Free has been described as "perfect American character ballet." In early 1944, Ballet Theatre (later American Ballet Theatre) commissioned Jerome Robbins and Leonard Bernstein, two new talents, to do a ballet for that spring. Jerome Robbins had studied all the choreographic methods, and was a comedian and dance soloist. He has contributed zany, satiric humor to dance and his choreography requires tremendous physical technique. A young designer, Oliver Smith, was asked by Robbins to design the set.

Leonard Bernstein went on a cross-country concert tour, Oliver Smith was in Mexico and Jerome Robbins was dancing with Ballet Theatre on the road, so the three kept in touch by telephone and by mail. In this long-distance manner, the creative elements of the ballet were brought together and it opened in April, 1944, with spectacular success. It was reviewed as a remarkable comedy with "witty and exuberant" dancers and pantomime. Jerome Robbins had succeeded in combining ballet and jazz dancing, the American folk dancing of the mid-twentieth century.

Fancy Free, created during the second World War, shows the concern of choreographic artists to bring dance forms and techniques together with the popular taste of the times. Diversionary entertainment had become popular since people needed something to take their minds off the war.

There is nothing especially "navy" about *Fancy Free,* even though the ballet concerns three sailors on shore leave. They are typical young men looking for girls and a good time. In that sense it is a timeless ballet, for the problem of young people seeking social contacts is similar in every period of history.

The setting of the ballet is in New York on a hot summer night. Three sailors arrive at a bar. It is clear by their behavior that they are good friends, looking for fun. They have a drink, go back to the street and wait for something to happen. An attractive girl comes along and each sailor tries to interest her in himself. A small fight breaks out. When the girl leaves, two of the sailors follow her.

The one left alone goes back into the bar, where he meets another cute girl. They have a drink, he tells her about his war experiences, and they dance together slowly. They are about to leave the bar, when the first two sailors return with their girl. It is apparent that the girls know one another. They begin to chat, ignoring the sailors. The sailors don't know how to resolve the problem of three guys and two gals, and so they stage a dance competition with the girls as judges. The girls argue with one another, trying to make a decision. The sailors argue with them, then with each other, and end up in another fight. They don't notice the girls leaving without them.

When they realize the situation, they straighten their uniforms trying to decide what to do next. When another very attractive girl comes along, they hesitate and try to stall one another. But when one sailor takes after her, the others follow. The cycle is eternal.

West Side Story

Musical comedy. Choreography by Jerome Robbins. Music by Leonard Bernstein. Book by Arthur Laurents. Lyrics by Stephen Sondheim. Costumes by Irene Sharaff. Lighting by Jean Rosenthal. Scenery by Oliver Smith. First presented in New York City, 1957.

The dance training of many American choreographers has not been restricted to the classic style. They have studied the modern dance methods of Martha Graham and others who have contributed expressive movements to dance vocabulary. The different styles interact and sometimes merge. Ballet still stresses point work, *pirouettes* and elevation, and will probably retain what has remained strong and enduring over centuries. But new ideas have been added to the classic base. Formal acting, stances and bows have been replaced by more natural behavior.

Some American choreographers and classically trained dancers have become associated with the commercial theatre and are contributing to the development of a uniquely American dance style. Popular dancers, who previously learned only tap and acrobatic stunts, are now experts in several styles and can usually act and even sing.

In *Oklahoma!*, 1943, dancer and choreographer Agnes de Mille, was the first to use dancing for character development, dramatic atmosphere, and plot reinforcement in musical comedy. Her innovations have encouraged talented choreographers to work regularly in the musical comedy medium using ballet, modern dance and folk dance. The famous dream sequence from *Oklahoma!* demonstrated that dancing could say things more effectively than words.

Jerome Robbins' ballet *Fancy Free* was extended into the hit musical *On the Town,* which he also choreographed. This was followed by *High Button Shoes, The King and I* and others by Robbins. De Mille included long solo dances of sorrow in *Brigadoon* and *Carousel*, and the audience enjoyed dancing as a means of communication, not just as a diversion. Yet the performance with a message did not replace the lighter dances, but instead a balance was found for the continuing success of dance in musical comedy.

The story of Romeo and Juliet has inspired many choreographers to create successful musical dance combinations. Jerome Robbins chose the subject for the stage musical *West Side Story,* described as total theatre, where acting moves into dance and back. The story-ballet of dancing and drama includes the use of non-realistic dance pantomime. It is *ballet d'action* with dialogue. The movie version received the Critics Award as the best of 1961, and seven Oscars. Robbins was given the first Academy Award for Choreography. In making the film, Robbins made important progress in dance photography, an art in itself.

The characters in *West Side Story* parallel the characters in Romeo and Juliet. Two teen-aged gangs, one of Puerto Ricans (the Sharks) and the other of Irish and Italian West-Siders (the Jets) are led by Bernardo (Tybalt) and Riff (Mercutio) respectively. Fourteen-year-old Maria (Juliet) is in love with Tony (Romeo). She is a part of Bernardo's gang and Tony is one of the Jets. There is a street fight, a duel and an episode where Tony climbs up the drain pipe to Maria's fire-escape, the contemporary version of the balcony scene in Shakespeare's play. The action includes a competitive dance display in the school gym. There is a rumble, a battle that results in the deaths of the two gang leaders, one of whom is Maria's brother, killed by Tony. In the finale, the body of Tony, who was murdered in vengeance, is carried away in a procession by members of both gangs, accompanied by an anguished Maria.

Seven Brides for Seven Brothers

Hollywood musical comedy, 1954. Metro Goldwyn Mayer. Screenplay by Albert Hackett, Frances Goodrich, Dorothy Kingsley. Based on the story "Sobbin' Women" by Stephen Vincent Benét. Directed by Stanley Donen. Choreography by Michael Kidd. Music by Johnny Mercer. Lyrics by Gene de Paul. With Howard Keel, Jane Powell and Russ Tamblyn. Produced by Jack Cummings.

In early sound motion pictures in America, dance interludes were based mainly upon large groups of pretty girls arranged in geometric patterns or upon the individual dancing of solo stars. Successful ballet and musical comedy stars later appeared in movies and extended the range of entertainment possibilities still further.

One of the strongest types of dance movie is created when the star is actually a dancer, so that the dance sequences are not just a decorative incidental to the plot, but the main ingredient. The exceptional tap dancing of Fred Astaire, for example, has delighted millions of movie-goers. The dance sequences are finely interwoven with every aspect of the story, the dialogue, the pantomime and usually the courtship scenes.

Gene Kelly has also contributed his first-rate dancing and choreographic skills to motion picture dancing. He knows the potential of movies to create fantasy and spectacle, and takes advantage of the mobility of the camera to film details of dancing. He has stimulated interest in all forms of dance with his highly entertaining films. The popularity of the dance film has made it possible for many talented choreographers to explore new ideas.

The popular dance movie *Seven Brides for Seven Brothers* was produced in 1954. Michael Kidd, the choreographer, took advantage of the successful Broadway musical comedy format, making the dancing an integral part of the plot. It was a way to define characters, set moods and intensify events. Twelve of the fourteen principal characters were dancers.

The story is about seven Oregon farm boys who kidnap seven girls from a nearby town to be their brides. The screenplay was based on the story "Sobbin' Women" by Stephen Vincent Benét. Benét was an American poet, novelist and short story writer of the early 20th century who earned the Pulitzer Prize for his book-length poem of the Civil War, "John Brown's Body." His writings reveal a genuine passion for America and a deep interest in its folklore and its historical background. Benét's story was supposedly influenced by the legend of the Sabine women. The Sabines were an ancient people of central Italy whose women were kidnapped to supply wives for men in Rome.

Several formal dances are included in the movie, along with an acrobatic square dance and a tender dance for the brides. Action throughout the movie is choreographed. Dreamy dance is interwoven with the performance of farm chores by six of the brothers — chopping, sawing, and piling wood — to communicate the various thoughts in their minds. A robust fight between the brothers and the boys in the town is in every way a real fight, but it has a definite plan and design, with every detail choreographed.

The Red Shoes

English movie, 1948. In Technicolor with Moira Shearer and Anton Walbrook. Book by Emeric Pressburger. Art Direction by Hein Heckroth. Produced and directed by Emeric Pressburger and Michael Powell. Choreography for the ballet The Red Shoes within the movie, by Robert Helpmann, based on the tale by Hans Christian Andersen, with Moira Shearer as The Girl, Robert Helpmann as The Lover, and Leonide Massine as The Shoemaker. Original music by Brian Easdale.

Increasing public devotion and interest in ballet was apparent in the overwhelming success of *The Red Shoes*, an English film revolving around the career of a ballerina. The film played in one theatre in New York City alone for over a year! The spectacular ballet within the film was performed by Moira Shearer and Robert Helpmann, members of the Sadler's Wells Ballet (now the Royal Ballet) and Leonide Massine, who early in his distinguished career was a member of Diaghilev's Ballets Russes.

An immense amount of work and collaboration went into the creation of the movie. The plot of the film is concerned with the conflict a young dancer experiences in attempting to choose whether to pursue her own promising career or to sacrifice it for that of her husband, a composer, who wants her to give up the stage. The film reaches its climax in the ballet for which the dancer's husband has written the musical score.

The plot of this ballet within the film is based on Hans Christian Andersen's fable of the little girl who is bewitched by her red dancing shoes. The author of the film says that the ballet grew out of Andersen's story, and the main plot grew out of the ballet. The ballet is fourteen and a half minutes long.

The first scene takes place in the public square where The Girl longs for a pair of beautiful red shoes seen in The Shoemaker's window. The Lover tries to discourage her, sensing their magic properties, but The Shoemaker presents them to her. The Girl puts them on and dances off to the fair.

At the fair she dances with one partner after another, none of whom can keep up with the flashing red shoes. The Lover is lost but The Shoemaker remains behind her. The Girl goes back to the square, exhausted. She wants to rest but the shoes force her to go on. At this point she recognizes The Shoemaker as the symbol of her own ambition and her life in the ballet becomes confused with her real life in the larger film story.

In the final sequence The Girl returns to the village square. A priest bars her way into the church where she wants to repent of her vanity. She dies of exhaustion and the priest removes her shoes. He takes her body into the church while The Shoemaker replaces the red shoes in his window to attract his next victim.

This film has been described as the most perfect blending of the arts of motion picture and ballet ever achieved. The enchantment of the ballet with its elusive beauty is captured on film and is used to enhance the film's story. The screen ballet is another opportunity to enjoy the spectacle of the dance with greater occasion for special effects in color, fantasy, close-ups and focus on detail.

Always an international art form, ballet no longer has one city for its world capital. The important centers of activity shift with the finest teachers and the finest dancers. In addition to American Ballet Theatre and New York City Ballet, New York is home to the Joffrey Ballet, the Alvin Ailey Dance Theatre, the companies of Martha Graham, Merce Cunningham and others.

Most of the companies reflect the vision of one resident choreographer who provides new works and restages existing ballets. Those who enjoy ballet, ballet enthusiasts or balletomanes, are not content to see only familiar works. They expect new choreography on a regular basis.

The dance audience is enjoying explosive growth all across North America. The majority of the performances and the audiences are outside of New York. Greater support for ballet has made it possible for good dance to exist in all regions and most cities, well within reach of performers and audiences. There is a diversity of dance to be enjoyed. The traditions of classic ballet endure and the dance form will flourish wherever there are good teachers, choreographers, artists, composers, talented dancers and audiences who thrill to the beauty of the precise art that began in the court ballrooms of Italy and France five hundred years ago.